helyn's healthy kitchen

whole food, plant-based, nutrient-dense

smoothies
to live for!

by HELYN DUNN

ISBN 10: 0980070562
ISBN 13: 978-0-9800705-6-9

Published by Prominent Books, LLC

Prominent Books and the Prominent Books logo are property of Prominent Books, LLC.

Prominent Books

for Mikey...

my partner,
my biggest fan,
my best friend,
a self-proclaimed,
die-hard smoothie lover,
and a true connoisseur
of healthy foods.

Table of Contents

introduction

I'm glad you're reading this book. It means you care about your heath and are willing to seek out new recipes that will enhance your well-being and promote disease-free longevity. Welcome aboard! This is the first in a series of books ... to Live For!

You'll notice that on the cover of this book, there is the term "nutrient dense." This means that these smoothies don't just taste phenomenal; they're also loaded with nutrients that your body needs and with which can flourish. Eating well doesn't just mean "being vegan" although that is a big part of how I got started eating plant-based foods. Let's be honest ... french fries are vegan, so is white bread and Oreo cookies. Are they healthy? Certainly not. What's really important is the nutrient density of your foods. I am all about eating and promoting foods that give us a big nutrient bang for their caloric buck. I'm hoping that you will begin to enjoy these mouth-watering smoothies as an introduction to how great healthy foods can taste.

I first began eating nutrient dense foods in order to fix some things that were non-optimum with my health. My blood pressure was out the roof, as were my triglycerides and cholesterol levels. I was 40 pounds overweight and having bouts of bursitis—so bad that I was bedridden for weeks at time. Drugs were simply NOT the answer for me. I knew, with every fiber of my being, that was not the road I wanted to travel. So I began doing extensive research into nutrition and decided to completely eliminate all processed foods, all animal foods (including red meat, chicken, fish, eggs, and dairy), sugar, oil, and salt. Was it extreme? Some people thought so. But I think triple bypass surgery is more extreme!

Within only SIX weeks, my blood work was perfect. Not better. Perfect. I had lost 20 pounds, and my blood pressure came down substantially. FOOD IS POWERFUL. Everything you put in your mouth will either harm you or help you. There is no middle ground. We are creatures of habit, and changing the way we eat is difficult. I won't sugarcoat that fact. Our taste buds are so overwhelmed by the concentrated sugar, salt, and oil in processed foods that it takes time for them to readjust and be able to taste the true goodness that nature has provided for us in the form of whole foods—fruits, veggies, whole grains, beans, nuts, and seeds. But, if you do decide to dive in and change the way you are used to eating, cold turkey, it really only takes about two weeks for your tastes to change. You will be amazed at the nuances of flavors that you've been missing!

I started a plant-based, whole food blog called "Helyn's Healthy Kitchen" in late 2012 as I was excited to share some recipes I was creating and enjoying. It took off like a rocket! I welcome you to peruse all of my recipes at www.helynskitchen.com.

Smoothies are an amazing place to start a healthier lifestyle. Are you ready to experience more vitality? Better sleep? Increased mental clarity? Less illness, and an overall sense of well-being? Let's do this together with some delicious, nutritious Smoothies to Live For!

tools of the smoothie trade

Speaking of blending ... I am totally and completely biased, so don't even try to talk to me about ANY other blender but a Vitamix! I think if there were ever a fire in my home, instead of grabbing my purse, my jewelry, or cherished family photos, I would run for my Vitamix. I use mine at least once per day. Of course I use it for my smoothies, but it's also fabulous for soups, salad dressings, cashew cheeses, and so many other recipes. It is truly indispensable. Is it expensive? You bet. Is it worth every penny? Absolutely.

the vitamix 7500

Simply put, the quality of your blender will make or break your smoothie. So don't skimp on this one and only tool that you need to make the best smoothies on the block. And the Vitamix company is one of the best for customer service. They will take care of anything that goes wrong with your blender, no questions asked. Not that anything will. The Vitamix is a real workhorse.

smoothie basics

Besides having a good blender, one of the most important parts of a healthful smoothie is using pure ingredients. You should strive for natural and organic products, especially when using fruits and berries as they are some of the most heavily sprayed foods and we sure don't want to consume pesticides when embarking on a healthy diet.

When blending a smoothie, always start off with the liquid ingredients and add your solid/frozen ingredients a bit at a time to get an even blend and to make sure your blender's motor doesn't overheat ... be kind to your blender, and it will last a long time!

FRESH vs. FROZEN: many people say that fresh fruits are more healthful than frozen. I'm not so sure about that. For one thing, unless you grow your own fruit, you can be sure that what you're eating is not vine ripe. Most fruits are picked long before ripening in order to ensure their safe and bruise-free passage from wherever they're being shipped. They also are picked early so that by the time they reach the supermarket shelves, they're not overripe.

Frozen fruit, on the other hand, is more likely to be ripe when it's flash frozen. I use mostly frozen-purchased fruits in my smoothies, other than bananas, which I always try to find discounted in the paper bags at the supermarket. They're "strays" ... as my produce guy calls them. Single bananas (some a bit overripe) that most people won't buy because they want to buy a bunch, connected. Isn't that silly? I thought so.

Over time, when you've mastered some of these smoothie recipes, you will surely come up with your own concoctions ... flavors and textures that you prefer. Mix and match veggies and fruits, frozen and fresh, and create your own masterpieces!

liquid bases

There are many liquid options for you to chose from for your smoothie bases. One that I enjoy often is pure coconut water. It adds a hint of sweetness and a good dose of naturally-occurring electrolytes without adding too much flavor of its own. So you will see coconut water frequently on my ingredient lists, especially in the fruity smoothies.

Here is a list of options for smoothie bases:
* pure water
* coconut water
* soy milk
* rice milk
* hemp milk
* cashew milk
* almond milk
* Brazil nut milk
* macadamia nut milk
* herbal teas
* coffee/coffee substitutes
* fruit juices
* vegetable juices

add-ins

Here is where some nutritional savvy comes in. You can take a "plain old smoothie" and really amp up its nutrient profile by having on hand and using a wide variety of superfood add-ins such as:

* flax seeds
* hemp seeds
* chia seeds
* wheat grass juice/powder, spirulina, etc.
* maca powder
* lucuma powder
* cacao powder/nibs
* bee pollen
* goji berries
* raw nuts and nut butters
* turmeric

flax seeds:

Flax seeds have been established and widely accepted as beneficial to our health in so many ways. The most popular of its health benefits are the omega-3 fatty acids that it provides. The primary omega-3 fatty acid found in flaxseeds is alpha-linolenic acid, or ALA, which can help protect the blood vessels from inflammation—an important factor in promoting a healthy cardiovascular system. Protection of our blood vessels from inflammatory damage is also provided by the lignans in flaxseeds. These lignans can inhibit formation of platelet activating factor (PAF), which increases the risk of inflammation when produced in excessive amounts.

Intake of flax seeds has also been shown to decrease the ratio of LDL-to-HDL cholesterol in several human studies. This HDL-related benefit may be partly due to the simple fiber content of flaxseeds, since 2 tablespoons of ground flaxseed provides about 4 grams of dietary fiber.

The antioxidant and anti-inflammatory benefits of flaxseeds also make them a good candidate for cancer prevention. That's because chronic inflammation (even low level inflammation) and chronic oxidative stress are risk factors for cancer development.

There are many other documented benefits to adding flax seeds to your diet. It only makes sense to include some on a daily basis. As you will see, I use flax in many of my smoothie recipes.

hemp seeds:

The first thing I want to point out is that hemp is not the same as marijuana. Although marijuana and hemp come from the same genus and species of plant, the varieties used in plant breeding are different, and hemp contains only very tiny amounts of THC, which is the psychoactive compound found in marijuana.

Hemp seeds have a concentrated balance of easily-digested proteins, essential fats, vitamins, and enzymes combined with a relative absence of sugar, starches, and saturated fats. Hemp protein is also a complete source of all 20 known amino acids including the 9 essential amino acids (EAAs) which our bodies cannot produce.

Adding hemp seeds to a smoothie adds a wonderful creaminess and a bit of a nutty flavor.

chia seeds:

Ch-ch-ch-chia! No longer just for chia pets, chia seeds are a true superfood loaded with health-promoting omega-3 fatty acids—nearly five grams in a one-ounce serving! They are also an excellent source of fiber at 10 grams per ounce (about 2 tablespoons) and contain protein and minerals including iron, calcium, magnesium, and zinc. Chia also assists in weight loss as well as reducing glucose levels, which can certainly benefit diabetics.

Check out these phenomenal statistics. Ounce-for-ounce, chia seeds have:

* 100% more POTASSIUM than bananas
* 300% more SELENIUM than flax seed
* 1400% more MAGNESIUM than broccoli
* 200% more IRON than spinach
* 100% more DIETARY FIBER than bran flakes
* 50% more PROTEIN than kidney beans
* 500% more CALCIUM than milk and
* 600% more OMEGA 3 than salmon!

Chia seeds will add a LOT of thickness to smoothies as they become quite gelatinous. So a little goes a long way.

wheatgrass juice/powder, barley grass, spirulina, etc:

I don't often use these greens in my smoothies because I prefer fresh greens like kale, spinach and collards, but feel free to experiment with them yourself. They all contain high levels of chlorophyll, which is in itself a powerful blood purifier and healing agent. These greens are high in antioxidants and bioavailable micronutrients. Barley grass has been known to be a strong detoxifier, especially in conjunction with activated charcoal. You will need a special type of juicer of you're going to use fresh grass juices instead of powders. Grass extracts have a strong flavor, so start out with a little if you're adding it to your smoothie.

maca powder

What's so special about maca, and what is it exactly? Maca is often referred to as the "Ancient Superfood of the Incas" since it is grown in the Andes mountains and dates back to about 3800 B.C. Peruvian Indians cultivated and ate it for its nutritional and medicinal value. It's a cruciferous root vegetable with many powerful, health promoting properties.

Maca contains high amounts of minerals, vitamins, enzymes, and all of the essential amino acids. Also, being rich in B-vitamins, it's a great source of B-12 for vegans! It has high levels of bioavailable calcium and magnesium which helps in the remineralization of bone.

Some of the most popular attributes of maca root are its ability to balance hormones, increase fertility, and enhance sexual function. Instead of providing external sources of hormones to the body, maca works as an adaptogen, which means that it responds to different bodies' needs differently. If you're producing too much of a particular hormone, maca can help regulate the production downward. If you're producing too little, it can regulate the production upward.

lucuma powder

Lucuma powder is made from the subtropical fruit of the Pouteria lucuma tree, native to South America. It's naturally sweet, has a subtle maple flavor and is chock-full of nutrients including trace minerals, beta carotene, niacin, and iron and is also rich in protein, antioxidants, and fiber.

cacao powder/nibs

Cacao, or cocoa, has all of the health benefits of solid chocolate, minus the fat. In fact, cocoa powder can contain up to 10% of its weight in flavonoids and contains more antioxidants and flavonoids than any other food! Antioxidants have the power to reverse cellular damage, and flavonoids have been proven to improve circulation and reduce blood pressure ... Life is good!

Make sure that you purchase NON-ALKALIZED cocoa powder. What is the difference between alkalized and non-alkalized cocoa powder? Alkalized cocoa is also sometimes referred to as "Dutched" or "Dutch processed." Dutch processed cocoa is treated with an alkali, which helps neutralize cocoa's natural bitterness and acidity. The alkalization process produces a powder that is typically darker and redder than naturally processed cocoa.

Don't assume, however, that darker color implies deeper flavor.

Alkalized cocoa is typically milder in flavor than naturally processed cocoa. Non alkalized cocoa still contains the cocoa's natural acids. When the cocoa is processed with alkali in Dutch processing, the flavonoids are substantially reduced. Cacao nibs are never processed and are raw.

bee pollen

Bee pollen, as opposed to honey, is not truly an animal product as it comes from the flowers of the plants. However, it is "animal sourced". So, based on your own evaluation of the process whereby the pollen is obtained, you may choose to eat it or omit it from your diet if you are a strict vegan.

That said, bee pollen is an excellent source of many health-promoting substances. It contains a dozen amino acids, iron, and B-vitamins as well as vitamins C and E, and flavonoids. Bee pollen is also an excellent source of protein (35-40 percent). It has also been used with success in treating seasonal allergies as it reduces histamine in the body.

Here is a staggering fact: each bee pollen pellet contains over two million flower pollen grains, and one teaspoonful contains over 2.5 billion grains of flower pollen.

goji berries

Goji berries are one of my favorite superfoods. And for so many reasons...

prevent vision loss:

According to a study published in the 2005 issue of the British Journal of Nutrition, goji berries contain properties that prevent the risk of vision loss. Researchers at Hong Kong Polytechnic University fed 14 healthy volunteers a serving of 15 grams of goji berries daily for 28 days while comparing their blood levels to 13 control volunteers. After 28 days, the volunteers who consumed the fruits experienced significantly raised zeaxanthin levels in the blood (zeaxanthin is an antioxidant present in goji berries that helps preserve eyesight). Therefore, if you're suffering from poor or deteriorating eyesight, consider adding more goji berries to your diet.

NOTE: Here's an amazing personal win ... I have been eating nutrient-dense foods for about two years now. I recently went to the eye doctor because I needed a new prescription for my contact lenses. I also felt like my glasses prescription was too strong. Turns out my vision has improved MARKEDLY! My new prescription is more than one diopter lower than my last one! If you wear glasses or contacts, you will understand that one diopter is nothing to sneeze at ... maybe it was all those goji berries! :)

nutrient density:

Though goji berries are best known for their antioxidant activity, they also contain an impressive number of vitamins and minerals. According to Paul Gross in his report, "The Top 20 Superfruits," a quarter cup of goji berries contains 11 essential vitamins and 22 trace minerals, including 24 percent RDI (recommended daily intake) of potassium, 18 percent RDI of zinc, and a whopping 100 percent of our RDI of iron, copper, and riboflavin. They also contain 8 polysaccharides, a primary source of dietary fiber.

better sleep:

Consumption of goji berries daily can improve sleep patterns. In a study published by the Journal of Complementary and Alternative Medicine, participants consuming goji reported better sleep, woke refreshed, and had higher energy levels than people who were taking a placebo. Goji berries are a rich source of magnesium and thiamin (B1), both of which are necessary for healthful sleep. And here's a very interesting fact about goji berries: they contain naturally occurring melatonin! So have some before bed for a restful night's sleep.

raw nuts and nut butters

The addition of nuts and nut butters result in super creamy, dreamy smoothies. They also add a dose of plant-strong protein. Keep in mind that nuts, while very beneficial in moderation, are high in fat. So if you're on a quest to lose weight, limit them.

turmeric

Another wonder of nature is turmeric. It's that very bright yellow-orange herbal root that makes curries and mustard yellow. Turmeric is part of the ginger family and has been a staple in Middle Eastern and Southeast Asian cooking for thousands of years. But there's a lot more to this vivid root than meets the eye. It is known to be one of the most powerfully healing herbs on the planet....

Doctors at UCLA recently found that curcumin, the main component in turmeric, appeared to block an enzyme that promotes the growth of head and neck cancer. In that study, 21 subjects with head and neck cancers chewed two tablets containing 1,000 milligrams of curcumin. An independent lab in Maryland evaluated the results and found that the cancer-promoting enzymes in the patients' mouths were inhibited by the curcumin and thus prevented from advancing the spread of the malignant cells.

Numerous other studies have determined that turmeric is one of the most potent, natural anti-inflammatories available in food form, resulting in significant reduction in arthritis symptoms.

smoothies vs. fresh juicing

I know many people assert that juicing is the best way to regain health, but I beg to differ. While juicing fresh fruits and vegetables is certainly better than drinking soda and processed juices, there is one rather big exclusion in that glass of juice that is vital to health ... FIBER. The importance of dietary fiber simply cannot be understated when desiring to achieve optimal health. From controlling blood sugar, to weight loss, heart health, and gut health, fiber is essential. Smoothies retain ALL of the fiber in the foods for a complete "meal in a glass."

What about all those micronutrients that are abundantly extracted by juicing? You may be surprised to know that by juicing instead of blending, many of those health-promoting benefits can be substantially decreased! Many beneficial micronutrients are often bound to the large molecules within the plant cells, including fiber, proteins, and starches. Chewing does not necessarily break down these fibers, and so blending is a great way to ensure their optimum absorption. But those micronutrients that are bound to fibers within the plant cell can often be removed with the fiber by juicing.[1]

One of the other concerns about juicing is the potential for overloading the pancreas with a jolt of natural sugars, especially from fruits, carrots, and beets. Blending, however, preserves the insoluble fiber of the fruits or veggies. Insoluble fiber slows down the body's ability to uptake sugar, which in turn prevents blood sugar spikes.

Juices also often leave one in a caloric deficit. If you're replacing a meal with juice, chances are you're going to be very hungry in short order. When blending, you can add many nutritious and satisfying ingredients that you wouldn't be able to juice, such as nuts and seeds and other superfoods. You can even add beans to your smoothie! I know, it sounds strange, but I've had a few smoothies with pinto beans that were delicious. Bottom line, you'll be more satiated with a smoothie as a meal.

I'm not saying that you should never have a brilliant glass of fresh green juice, or a yummy carrot/apple/beet combo juice. Moderation is key, and try to enjoy your juice with a meal of solid foods to avoid a sugar spike, or cut the juice with some water. I sometimes will use fresh carrot juice as a base for soups, which adds a tremendous amount of flavor and additional nutrients. So be sensible about juicing!

---

[1] Parada J, Aguilera JM: Food microstructure affects the bioavailability of several nutrients. *J Food Sci* 2007, 72:R21-32.

what about nuts and seeds?

There are some schools of nutritional thought which shun nuts and seeds due to their high fat content. Yes, they are high in fats, although they are "healthy" fats. But it's not the fat content of a diet that makes it healthy, it's the nutrient content. And, based on their nutrient content, nuts are a health-promoting source of calories.

Nuts and seeds are a natural part of the diet of Homo sapiens. Study after study shows that raw nuts and seeds not only lower cholesterol but protect against the common degenerative diseases of aging. Although nuts and seeds offer so many health benefits, it is important to adjust their consumption depending on your activity level as well as weight loss goals. A handful of nuts is a good gauge as a daily portion for most people.

There is also something very special about the synergistic effect of nuts and seeds with greens and other fruits and vegetables. Some vitamins, minerals, and micronutrients require dietary fat to be absorbed into the body and to do their jobs, which include providing energy, keeping cells functioning, and supporting the immune system, for a start. When fat-soluble vitamins are ingested, they move from the mouth to the stomach to the small intestine. Their ability to dissolve in fat allows for their absorption. Dietary fats carry the vitamins through the intestine, into the bloodstream, and then to the liver, where they're stored until the body needs them. Without an adequate amount of fat in your diet, your body is unable to effectively absorb the fat-soluble vitamins that are essential to your health.

Of course, the KIND of fat you eat is just as important as getting some in your diet. Raw nuts, seeds, and avocado are the best sources of dietary fat and will help your body assimilate all of those critical nutrients in your smoothies! So add a handful of nuts or seeds to your smoothie or eat them on the side if you prefer. But remember, a little goes a long way unless you're a marathon runner!

a short history of smoothies

As a "foodist," I am always so curious as to the origin of certain recipes and culinary delights. Where did the first "smoothie" originate? Well, it seems that the sweet sensation known as the Indian "lassi" is the winner, with the first known lassi dating back to somewhere around 1,000 BC. Lassis are traditionally made with fresh fruits, spices, and cultured milk or yogurt and have been prized across South Asia for their great taste & healing Ayurvedic properties.

Health food stores of the West Coast of the United States began selling puréed fruit drinks in the 1930s based on recipes that originated in Brazil. Some historians credit the word "smoothie" to describe a blended fruit drink as having originated with hippies in the 1960s, which is rather poetic and fun. But in the 1940s, waring blendor cookbooks were published with recipes for banana and pineapple smoothies. The first trademark for a fruit slush was in the mid-1970s with the name "California Smoothie," which was marketed by the California Smoothie Company.

In the 1970s, a lactose intolerant man by the name of Steven Kuhnau began to create fruit smoothies to be able to enjoy something similar to the milkshakes most of his friends liked. Not only did he love the flavor, but he realized that his smoothie creations were helping to control his blood sugar levels and food allergies as well! Steven went on to open his first health food store, calling his drinks "smoothies", thinking that the local hippies would know what they were. So there must be some truth to the hippie story! He thereafter founded the well-known smoothie chain, "Smoothie King," now having more than 600 stores nationwide.

Peace!

summing up

As you can clearly see, there is much more to a healthy smoothie than merely satisfying a sweet tooth or a craving for dessert. Smoothies have gained much popularity within the health conscious community for a reason. Fast, easy, nutrient-rich and oh so tasty! There are innumerable combinations of ingredients that you can mix and match to suit your taste while incorporating superfoods into the recipes if you so choose. Smoothies are the perfect way to start your day, enjoy as a healthy snack or to add nutrients to any meal. Yes, it's all about the nutrients. So without further ado ... let's get started!

fruity smoothies

pretty in pink raspberry smoothie

Helyn's notes: As much as you may love berries, make sure to buy only organic to avoid harmful pesticide residues. Berries are one of the most heavily sprayed fruits out there!

ingredients:

- 2 cups frozen organic raspberries
- 2 cups unsweetened, plant-based milk or other non-dairy beverage
- 4 pitted medjool dates
- 6 large ice cubes
- 1/4 cup raw cashews
- 2 TBSP raw hemp seeds

procedure:

1. Place the cashews, dates, and 1 cup of the milk into a high-powdered blender and blend until smooth.
2. Add remaining ingredients and blend until smooth.
3. Chances are you will wind up with some of the cashew mixture at the bottom that didn't totally blend with the rest of the smoothie ingredients, which makes for a very lovely presentation on top when the smoothie is poured into glasses.

Serves 2

sweet

deep purple smoothie

Helyn's notes: Not many ingredients are in this smoothie, but the flavor is amazing ... its sweetness is obtained from the grapes. Wait until it's grape season for this one to get the best black grapes. The rich color of this smoothie is phenomenal due to all of those anthocyanins ... antho-who? Anthocyanins are the water-soluble pigments found in foods such as blueberries, cherries, and many other plant-based foods.

Black grapes are absolutely loaded with anthocyanins. Based upon many studies and human clinical trials, it has been suggested that anthocyanins possess anti-inflammatory and anti-carcinogenic activity, prevent cardiovascular disease, control obesity, and alleviate diabetes, all of which are more or less associated with their potent antioxidant properties. Drink up!

ingredients:

- 2 cups frozen black grapes (seedless and organic)
- 2 cups frozen blueberries
- 4 large kale leaves
- 1 ½ cups coconut water
- 2 TBSP flax meal

procedure:

Blend and enjoy!

Serves 2

mango lassi smoothie

Helyn's notes: If you've ever had a mango lassi at an Indian restaurant, you know how good they are. Lassis are traditional yogurt based drinks, which originated in the Punjab region of South Asia, spanning India and Pakistan. While I've always enjoyed mango lassis, especially with a hot Indian dish, I found them to be too sweet due to the added sugar that is usually used.

This smoothie contains the simplest of ingredients and no added sugar (the coconut water adds just the right amount of sweetness, especially if your mangos are sweet). And instead of yogurt, I used coconut milk. You could certainly replace the coconut milk with a soy yogurt to have a more authentic, slightly sour flavor if you like, keeping it vegan.

ingredients:

- 1 pound mango, cubed and frozen. When mangos are readily available, I usually buy a lot and freeze them. They're great in all kinds of smoothies. And it's a lot cheaper to freeze your own. For this particular smoothie, I just used a one-pound bag of frozen mango from my grocer's freezer.
- 1 15-oz. can coconut water
- 3 TBSP coconut milk
- 1 carrot
- dash of Garam Masala for garnish (or you could use cinnamon, nutmeg and/or cloves)

procedure:

1. Place all ingredients into a high powered blender and blend until smooth.
2. Serve with a swirl of coconut milk, and garnish with spices of your choice.

Serves 2

blueberry bliss smoothie

Helyn's notes: Depending on how sweet (or not!) your berries are, you can always add a date or two to sweeten your smoothie. I didn't need to add any with this one.

ingredients:

- 16 oz. pomegranate-blueberry juice. Pom is the one I used, available in just about any grocery store. If you can find straight blueberry juice that is unsweetened, that would work as well or better!
- 1/2 cup raw cashews
- 3 cups fresh or frozen blueberries (I used frozen, which makes for a nice, cold smoothie)
- 1 packet frozen acai (find in health food stores)
- 1/4 cup raw hemp seeds

procedure:

1. Soak the goji berries in a little of the coconut water for about 15 minutes.
2. Add them and all remaining ingredients to your blender and blend until smooth.

Serves 2

blackberry basil smoothie

Helyn's notes: Who would have ever thought that basil would taste so good with berries? Well, basil is in the mint family after all, so it's not THAT weird. And my garden basil was getting so unruly, I thought I would try some in a smoothie. Yes! This one is a keeper.

ingredients:

- 2 frozen bananas
- 2 cups frozen blackberries
- 1 cup frozen mango chunks
- 2 cups coconut water
- 2 TBSP flax meal
- 1 TBSP maca powder
- handful of fresh basil leaves

procedure:

Blend and enjoy!

Serves 2

peachy keen smoothie

Helyn's notes: This is a wonderful summertime smoothie ... creamy and peachy with just the right sweetness to enjoy on a balmy day! The addition of maca powder amps up the nutritional profile, and the cashews add an extra dose of heart-friendly sterols, known to reduce LDL cholesterol, and an abundance of minerals.

ingredients:

- 1 frozen banana
- 4 fresh peaches, pits removed
- 2 cups unsweetened, plant-based milk
- 1/2 cup raw cashews
- 1 TBSP maca powder
- 1 tsp pure vanilla extract (optional)

procedure:

1. Blend the cashews and bananas with one cup of the milk until smooth.
2. Add the remaining ingredients.
3. Blend and enjoy!

Serves 2

...peachy

good morning

good morning sunshine smoothie

Helyn's notes: Here's a great way to wake up and start the day. Get a shot of energy from the freshness of this beautiful morning smoothie and a kick-ass serving of phytonutrients from those lovely goji berries. There's only one problem ... it's so pretty you may not want to drink it!

ingredients:

- 2 frozen bananas
- 1 cup frozen mango chunks
- 1 cup frozen watermelon chunks
- 1 cup frozen strawberries
- 1/4 cup goji berries
- 1 cup orange juice (preferably freshly squeezed)
- 1/2 cup coconut water

procedure:

1. Blend the goji berries with the coconut water until smooth.
2. Add the remaining ingredients.
3. Blend and enjoy!

Serves 2

power berry smoothie

Helyn's notes: Want a huge dose of health-promoting anthocyanins? Then this smoothie is for you! It's chock-full of berry goodness. Let's talk about those funny little goji berries for a moment. They are unique among other fruits because they contain all essential amino acids. Gojis also have the highest concentration of protein of any fruit. They're loaded with vitamin C, contain more carotenoids than any other food, have twenty-one trace minerals, and are high in fiber. Want more reasons to eat them? They have fifteen times the amount of iron found in spinach, as well as calcium, zinc, selenium and other important trace minerals.

ingredients:

- 1 10-oz. bag frozen strawberries (about 2 cups)
- 1 10-oz. bag frozen raspberries (about 2 cups)
- ½ cup goji berries
- 1½ cups coconut water
- ½ cup unsweetened, plant-based milk
- 1 TBSP hemp seeds
- 1 TBSP ground flax seeds
- 1 TBSP maca powder
- 2-4 pitted medjool dates (optional and depending on how sweet you prefer your smoothie and how sweet your berries are)

procedure:

1. Soak the goji berries in a little of the coconut water for about 15 minutes.
2. Add them and all remaining ingredients to your blender and blend until smooth.

Serves 2

piña colada smoothie ~ non-alcoholic

Helyn's notes: Have you ever enjoyed a piña colada cocktail? This smoothie is so luscious and luxuriously coconutty, you'll be in heaven if you're a fan of these popular tropical flavors. It's a cinch to make, too, with only four ingredients. You can use canned coconut milk for this, but I prefer to make my own. It's so simple to make, and the flavor is outstanding. See recipe below....

ingredients:

- 2 frozen bananas
- 1 1/2 cups frozen pineapple chunks
- 1 cup coconut water
- 1 cup coconut milk

for the coconut milk:

Ingredients:
- 2 cups unsweetened shredded coconut
- 3 cups pure coconut water

Procedure:
1. Blend in a high powdered blender for about one minute.
2. Strain through a nut bag (this step is crucial for a smooth milk).

procedure:

Blend and enjoy!

Serves 2

Enjoy the moment

superfruit sangria smoothie ~ non-alcoholic

Helyn's notes: My honey and I agree. This. Is. Hands down fabulously, amazingly, indisputably the best smoothie we have ever tasted. Seriously! Another non-alcoholic copycat for you (but frozen) and another smoothie you'll want to make when those black grapes and peaches are in season. Yowza! Yeah. Hell, yeah.

ingredients:

- 4 cups frozen black seedless grapes
- 2 cups frozen blueberries
- 2 cups sliced fresh peaches (not frozen)
- 1 TBSP pomegranate juice concentrate (I use Jarrow brand, hands down THE best one out there. I use it in many of my smoothies. It adds a huge dose of antioxidants and a nice tart richness to any smoothie. Find it in health food stores or online at Amazon or VitaCost.com)

procedure:

Blend and enjoy!

Serves 2

low-glycemic berry blast smoothie

Helyn's notes: All fruits are not off limits for diabetics. In fact, some berries have been studied and proven to be of benefit to those with type 2 diabetes ... For example, blueberries may help your body process glucose for energy efficiently, both increasing its sensitivity to insulin and managing blood sugar, which can help you fight diabetes.

A University of Michigan Cardiovascular Center study notes that laboratory rats that were fed blueberries crushed into a powder showed improved insulin sensitivity, even when eating a high-fat diet along with the blueberries. The coconut water in this recipe adds a bit more sweetness to the tart berries, but not too much. You can also use plain, pure water instead if your berries are nice and sweet.

ingredients:

- 1 cup frozen blueberries
- 1 cup frozen blackberries
- 1 cup frozen raspberries
- small handful frozen mango chunks
- 2 cups unsweetened, pure coconut water
- 3 kale leaves
- 2 TBSP flax meal

procedure:

1. Place all ingredients into a high-powdered blender and blend until smooth.
2. Serve topped with some fresh berries (they will eventually sink and it's fun to scoop them out at the end ... like finding hidden treasures!)

Serves 2

Did you know that type 2 diabetes is often reversible by simply changing one's diet and incorporating a moderate but frequent exercise program? The heavier a person is, the greater their chance of developing type 2 (also known as "adult onset") diabetes. The best diet for humans to live longer in superior health is also the best diet for reversing diabetes. It is not a low-carbohydrate or low-fat diet; it is a high-nutrient diet... one which focuses on the quality of carbohydrates, proteins, and fats; an eating style with a high micronutrient to calorie ratio. When one eats this way, it becomes relatively easy to quickly shed excess pounds without hunger or deprivation, and bring glucose numbers back down into the non-diabetic range. There is much evidence-based information available online and in books. I urge you to do you own research on the topic.

super blue smoothie

Helyn's notes: This is my go-to smoothie. It's the one I have most often above all others. It has a perfect balance of flavors ... not too sweet, not too tart, and offers a horde of nutrition for a great way to start any day.

ingredients:

- 1-2 frozen bananas (depending on how sweet you like it)
- handful of frozen mango, peaches or pineapple
- ½ pouch frozen acai berry (find in health food stores) or 1 cup frozen, diced watermelon
- 3-5 leaves of fresh kale (stems removed—you can also throw in some spinach or collards)
- 2 TBSP ground flax meal
- 1 can (17 oz) coconut water (find in health food stores)
- 1 TBSP maca powder
- 1 TBSP pomegranate juice concentrate
- 2 cups frozen blueberries

procedure:

1. Blend all ingredients, except blueberries, until smooth.
2. Add blueberries about a cup at a time and blend until smooth.

Serves 2

mine →

strawberry maca smoothie

Helyn's notes: This strawberry smoothie is creamy and scrumptious while being loaded with plant-strong nutrients and protein. Check out the information about maca powder in the front of the book if you haven't already. I love smoothies, and this one is so yummy, you can serve it to your children and they'll think they are drinking a strawberry milkshake. Go for it!

ingredients:

- 1 frozen banana
- 3 cups frozen strawberries
- 1 cup coconut water
- 1 cup unsweetened, plant-based milk
- 6 pitted medjool dates
- ¼ cup raw sunflower seeds
- 2 TBSP hemp seeds
- 1 TBSP raw maca powder

procedure:

1. Place all ingredients into a blender and blend until super smooth.
2. Top with a little extra hemp seeds and/or fresh strawberries if you like.

Serves 2

shakes

vanilla chai chia shake

Helyn's notes: If you like the taste of chai spices and enjoy cool, refreshing shakes, this is the beverage for you! The chia seeds not only make this a wonderfully thick shake, but also contribute all of their super health wonders. This shake is also loaded with plant-strong protein ... seeds, soy, and nut butter!

ingredients:

- 2 bananas
- 2 cups unsweetened, plant-based milk
- 6 ice cubes
- 1/2 cup raw almond butter
- 2 TBSP ground flax seeds
- 1 TBSP ground chia seeds
~ the spices
- 2 tsp cinnamon (plus more for garnish)
- 1/4 tsp cloves
- 1/2 tsp black pepper
- 1/2 tsp ground cardamom
- 1 tsp ground nutmeg

...OR if you have the spice blend called Garam Masala, you can simply use 1 TBSP of this blend plus one teaspoon of cinnamon in place of all the spices listed above.

procedure:

1. Blend until smooth.
2. Top with a sprinkle of cinnamon if you like.

Serves 2

cherries jubilee shake ~ alcohol-free

Helyn's notes: Cherries Jubilee is a dessert made of cherries in a cherry liqueur that is typically flambéed and served with vanilla ice cream. Well, this frozen drink is certainly not going to be flambéed, and there is also no alcohol ... I am calling it Cherries Jubilee because one of the definitions of "jubilee" (in a loose sense) is a celebration or festival.

Every day is worthy of celebration when you are treating your body to such healthy deliciousness! And this shake is certainly something to celebrate with its nourishing, sweet cherries, protein, rich hemp seeds, and smooth, ice-cream–like texture.

ingredients:

- 2 cups frozen sweet black cherries
- 2 frozen bananas
- 2 cups unsweetened, plant-based milk
- 2 TBSP hemp hearts
- 1 tsp pure vanilla extract

procedure:

Blend and enjoy!

Serves 2

strawberry guava shake

Helyn's notes: There are so many health benefits of guava, it is hard to know where to begin. It is important to know that guava helps control diabetes and protects the prostate. But recent studies have also shown it to be protective against high blood pressure, bacterial infections, and also aids in weight loss. It tastes great, too!

I found a great guava juice, Ceres brand, in my local supermarket, which contains only guava and pear juice. I have never been able to find fresh guava fruit that is tasty and ripe. If you can, then use it in this smoothie in place of the juice!

ingredients:

- 2 frozen bananas
- about 2 cups (1 10-oz. package) frozen strawberries
- 2 cups guava juice
- ½ cup unsweetened, plant-based milk
- 2 TBSP flax meal
- 2 TBSP hemp seeds
- 1-2 pitted medjool dates if you want it sweeter (I found it sweet enough without)

procedure:

Blend and enjoy!

Serves 2

oatmeal raisin cookie shake

Helyn's notes: Cookies in a glass! What a total treat this shake is! Especially if you have some oatmeal raisin cookies to crumble on top. Yippee! Drinking healthy never tasted so good.

ingredients:

- 2 frozen bananas
- 1 cup rolled oats
- 5 cups unsweetened, plant-based milk
- 1/2 cup organic raisins
- 1/4 cup raw almond butter
- 1 TBSP flax meal
- 1 tsp pure vanilla extract
- 1 tsp ground cinnamon

procedure:

Blend and enjoy!

Serves 2

love it ♡↓

strawberry banana shake

Helyn's notes: Strawberries and bananas have been friends for a long time. They complement one another … "My, don't you look nice today." Umm, not that kind of compliment. They just taste good together! And talk about easy? You could make this one in your sleep … bff! ♥

ingredients:

- 2 frozen bananas
- 2 cups strawberries (fresh or frozen)
- 2 cups unsweetened, plant-based milk

procedure:

1. Blend and enjoy!

Serves 2

mocha shake

Helyn's notes: Mmmmmmocha. Coffee and chocolate create such an earthy flavor combination. Of course, I don't drink coffee, but I sometimes enjoy a yummy coffee alternative called Dandy Blend. It's made from roasted chicory and tastes quite a lot like coffee, but it's not bitter, it doesn't make my heart race, and it's not addictive. Yeah. I'm good with that.

ingredients:

- 2 cups cashew milk, frozen in ice cube trays overnight
- 1 1/2 cups brewed coffee or coffee substitute (COLD)
- 6 ice cubes
- 2 TBSP flax meal
- 1 TBSP maca powder
- 2 TBSP cocoa powder
- 1/2 cup pitted medjool dates
- 1 tsp vanilla

procedure:

1. For the cashew milk, blend 1 cup raw cashews with 3 cups pure water. Refrigerate.
2. Blend all ingredients and enjoy!

Serves 2

apple pie shake

Helyn's notes: This shake is a cinch to make, and it is totally the bomb. Apple pie in a glass, please!

ingredients:

- 1 large apple, cored and rough chopped
- 2 frozen bananas
- 2 cups unsweetened, plant-based milk
- 4 pitted medjool dates
- 1 TBSP maca powder
- 1 TBSP lucuma powder
- 2 tsp cinnamon
- 2 tsp vanilla

procedure:

Blend and enjoy! Top with extra cinnamon, a cinnamon stick, and apple slices for a fancy presentation.

Serves 2

all gone.

pumpkin spice shake

Helyn's notes: Welcome the fall with this shake. Its pumpkin pie spices will tickle your taste buds and leave you with a dose of warm fuzzies ... even if it is a frozen drink!

ingredients:

- 1 cup pumpkin puree
- 2 frozen bananas
- 2 cups unsweetened, plant-based milk
- 2-4 pitted medjool dates, depending on your sweet tooth
- 2 tsp pumpkin pie spice

procedure:

Blend and enjoy!

Serves 2

lucuma walnut coffee shake

Helyn's notes: Good morning! This beverage is a wakeup call in the best of ways...
Nourishing and satisfying, you can call it breakfast with a side of plant-strong
nutrients.

ingredients:

- 2 frozen bananas
- 1 cup unsweetened, plant-based milk
- 1 cup brewed coffee or coffee substitute (COLD)
- ½ cup raw walnuts
- 6 pitted medjool dates
- 2 TBSP flax meal
- 2 TBSP lucuma powder
- 1 cup ice

procedure:

Blend and enjoy!

Serves 2

kreamy kiwi shake

Helyn's notes: Kiwiiiiiiis. Did you know that these fuzzy little fruits are tremendous storehouses of nutrition? They are loaded with micronutrients and have specific health benefits with regard to childhood asthma and allergies—a study in Italy indicated that children had less trouble with wheezing, shortness of breath, and coughing in the night when they consumed 5–7 servings of kiwi per week.

Adults can also benefit from eating kiwis. Another study demonstrated that eating 2–3 kiwi fruits a day can reduce the potential for blood clots and decrease triglycerides. Yet another study cited the kiwi's ability to protect and repair the body from DNA damage, which could protect against cancer. Oh, my. Let's get blending!

ingredients:

- 4 kiwis
- 2 seedless oranges
- 1/4 cup raw Brazil nuts
- 2 cups coconut water
- 4 TBSP raw hemp seeds
- 2 pitted medjool dates
- handful of mild-tasting greens, such as spinach or lettuce

procedure:

1. Place the Brazil nuts and 1/2 cup coconut water in a high powered blender and blend until the nuts are very smooth.
2. Peel the oranges and add to the blender whole with all remaining ingredients EXCEPT the kiwis. Blend until smooth.
3. Peel the kiwis and add to the blender. Blend on LOW until just mixed. The reason I add the kiwis last and don't blend a lot is because it's really nice to have those little black kiwi seeds stay whole! Adds a little crunch and texture.
4. Garnish with some extra kiwi and orange slices if you like.

Serves 2

chocolate cherry shake

Helyn's notes: Kids, young and old, will love the creamy, rich, chocolatey goodness of this nutrient—dense smoothie, infused with the distinct flavor of sweet cherries! Cocoa powder has all of the health benefits of solid chocolate, minus the fat. In fact, cocoa powder can contain up to 10% of its weight in flavonoids and contains more antioxidants and flavonoids than any other food! Life is good.

ingredients:

- 2 frozen bananas
- 2 cups fresh or frozen pitted black cherries
- 4 pitted medjool dates
- 1 TBSP flax meal
- handful of fresh kale (no, you cannot taste them in here, I promise!)
- 1 cup unsweetened, plant-based milk
- 1/2 cup unsweetened cherry juice or coconut water
- 2 TBSP unsweetened, non-alkalized (or raw) cocoa powder

procedure:

Blend and enjoy!

Serves 2

pistachio shake

Helyn's notes: Raise your hand if you love pistachio ice cream! This is the epitome of an old-fashioned milk shake with the rich, nutty flavor of pistachios! Compared to other nuts, pistachios contain large amounts of antioxidants, beta-carotene, vitamin E and lutein, which is a naturally occurring carotenoid (plant pigment) that benefits eye health. They are also lower in calories than other nuts and are loaded with flavor and healthy fats.

ingredients:

- 2 frozen bananas
- 1/2 cup raw shelled pistachios
- 1/4 cup raw cashews
- 1 avocado
- 1 cup fresh spinach
- 2 cups unsweetened, plant-based milk
- 2 drops pure almond extract (really, all you need is 2 drops!)
- 2 pitted medjool dates
- squeeze of fresh lemon juice

procedure:

Blend and enjoy!

Serves 2

FUN FACT:
Ever wonder why pistachios are green? As the pistachio nut grows, it expands until it pops its shell open (lucky for us, it makes them easier to get to!) The nut is then exposed to the sun and creates chlorophyll, just like any other green plant!

super "q" chocolate shake

Helyn's notes: In physics, "Q" is the symbol for heat energy or electrical charge. I'm calling this a "Super Q" shake because it will supercharge your engine! There are so many natural, energizing ingredients in this drink that it's perfect for a fast start to a busy day. If you're a chocolate lover (like me) you will love the rich, dense flavors that linger on your taste buds. VROOOOM!

ingredients:

- ¼ cup raw almond butter
- ¼ cup cacao nibs (or non-alkalized cocoa powder)
- 3 TBSP non-alkalized cocoa powder
- 6 pitted medjool dates
- 1 cup brewed Kukicha tea, cooled
- ½ cup unsweetened, plant-based milk
- 2-3 kale leaves, thick inner stems removed
- 1 TBSP vanilla extract
- 2 TBSP flax meal
- 2 TBSP hemp seeds
- 1 tsp chia seeds
- 1 heaping tsp cinnamon
- 2 frozen bananas
- 1 cup frozen blueberries
- 4 ice cubes

procedure:

1. Place the cacao nibs, almond butter, dates, and milk substitute in your Vitamix and blend until smooth. The reason I add these ingredients first is because those cacao nibs can be a bit tough to break down and can add a little grit to the smoothie (not so pleasant). So you may need to blend them for a while. Adding the rest of the ingredients last ensures a smooth texture and a cold smoothie.
2. Add remaining ingredients and blend until smooth. Garnish with cocoa nibs and enjoy!

Serves 2

horchata shake

Helyn's notes: Have you ever tried horchata? It's a Mexican drink made with rice milk, sugar, and cinnamon. Yummers! Well, turning it into a shake is pretty easy—just freeze the rice milk first. I have extra ice cube trays lying around for just such purposes. This is a perfect drink to serve with a spicy Mexican meal. Olé!

ingredients:

- 2 cups rice milk, frozen in a tray (one tray is about 2 cups).
- 1 tray of plain ice cubes
- 10 pitted medjool dates
- 1/2 cup raw cashews
- 1/2 cup rice milk, unfrozen
- 2 tsp ground cinnamon
- pinch of ground nutmeg

procedure:

1. Blend the cashews with the unfrozen rice milk.
2. Add the remaining ingredients.
3. Blend and enjoy!

Serves 2

Olé!

grasshopper shake ~ alcohol-free

Helyn's notes: When I became "of age", my dad used to order me Grasshoppers whenever we would go out to eat. He liked his alcohol and did not like to drink alone. They were pretty mild, being made with crème de menthe and, well, heavy cream. Of course, I loved them. They tasted like dessert! The mint and the cream were so refreshing, and this shake is even more so.

ingredients:

- 1 cup cashews
- 1 cup water
- 1 cup fresh peppermint leaves*
- 2 cups mache rosettes (or substitute baby spinach)
- ¼ cup sweetener of your choice (I used honey, which I rarely use but thought it would be nice in this drink. Yes, I am a "beegan"—a vegan who uses honey ... sometimes)
- 2 cups ice cubes

*NOTE: It can sometimes be hard to find fresh peppermint. Many grocery stores have mint, but it's usually spearmint and would change the flavor of this smoothie considerably. If you can't find fresh peppermint, substitute the mint leaves with 1 tsp of peppermint extract.

procedure:

1. Place the cashews and the water in a high-powered blender and blend until smooth.
2. Add all remaining ingredients and blend again until smooth.
3. Top with a sprig of fresh mint and enjoy!

Serves 2

orange creamsicle shake

Helyn's notes: Growing up on Long Island, in the summer months, I would listen attentively for the familiar sound of the bells on the neighborhood ice cream truck. I was often seduced by the infamous orange creamsicle! I've seen creamsicle smoothie recipes online, but most of them use ice cream or yogurt, and the vegan recipes use tofu or highly processed dairy-free frozen concoctions. So, here it is—a whole food, creamy, refreshing, cold one!

ingredients:

- 3 cups COLD orange juice (fresh squeezed is best!)—pop it in the freezer for a while if you want an extra cold and thick smoothie.
- 1 cup raw cashews
- ½ - 1 cup ice
- 3 pitted medjool dates
- 1 TBSP ground chia seeds
- 1 TBSP vanilla extract

procedure:

1. Place cashews in a high powdered blender and add just enough orange juice to cover. Blend until smooth.
2. Add the rest of the juice and remaining ingredients, and blend again until smooth.
3. Garnish with some fresh oranges and orange zest.

Serves 2

green drinks

hard core green smoothie

Helyn's notes: I was inspired to create this green smoothie while reading Victoria Boutenko's book *Green for Life*. In it, she talks of how she spent years researching chimps and their natural diets and how chimps and humans are so physiologically similar, sharing a whopping 99.4% of our DNA sequences. As it turns out, chimps eat a diet of predominantly GREENS and FRUITS. I thought they ate mostly bananas and insects! Victoria and her family had been on a raw food diet for years, but she felt something was missing. So she discovered greens and started drinking green smoothies, with amazing results. It's a great read, and I recommend it!

ingredients:

- 2 frozen bananas
- 1 cup frozen mango
- ½ cup frozen pineapple
- 1 cup baby spinach
- 6 "dino" leaves (lacinato kale)
- 2 cups coconut water

procedure:

Blend and enjoy!

Serves 2

green mocha frappé

Helyn's notes: Yes, it is army green. No, you cannot taste the kale! Before I began my whole foods, plant-based eating, I was a coffee junkie. No kidding. I spent a lot of money at that popular coffee joint—I won't mention names—but they've been in a hot seat of late regarding GMOs! Anyway, my favorite thing to order there was a mocha frappe. Here's a healthy version!

ingredients:

- 2 TBSP coffee substitute such as Kaffree Roma or Dandy Blend, or if you are a coffee drinker just use one cup of strongly brewed coffee.
- 1 cup boiling water
- 1 cup cold, unsweetened plant-based milk
- 4 lacinato kale leaves, stems removed
- 2 TBSP cocoa powder
- 6 pitted medjool dates
- 2 TBSP raw hemp seeds
- 1 TBSP flax meal
- ½ tsp pure vanilla extract
- 12 large ice cubes

procedure:

1. Ahead of time, make the "coffee" using 2 TBSP of coffee substitute with 1 cup boiling water.
2. Cool completely in the fridge.
3. Place the dates in a blender and add just enough of the "coffee" to cover.
4. Blend until the dates are completely liquefied.
5. Add all remaining ingredients and blend until smooth.
6. Sprinkle with some cocoa nibs for garnish (optional)
7. Serve immediately!

Serves 2

emerald jewelius

Helyn's notes: I remember getting orange julius drinks at a mall where I worked for a time. I loved the foamy texture and the orangey tang in those drinks! To this day, their recipe is a tightly held secret, but I've heard wind that they use egg whites ... That may explain all that foaminess! This recipe achieves a wonderful texture as well, with a divine combination of flavors.

ingredients:

- 2 frozen bananas
- 1 cup raw cashews
- 2 cups orange juice (freshly squeezed is best!)
- 1 whole orange, peeled (make sure there are no seeds)
- 6 ice cubes
- handful of baby spinach
- 1 TBSP maca powder

procedure:

Blend and enjoy!

Serves 2

new day green smoothie

Helyn's notes: Every day is a new day! And if you begin your day with this smoothie, you can be sure you are giving your body some superior nutrition to carry you through to its end. Packed with greens in a tangy, sweet orange juice base, this smoothie provides excellent micronutrient content and a satisfying, fresh taste. Enjoy it with some raw nuts for better absorption of fat-soluble vitamins in the greens.

ingredients:

- 2 cups orange juice
  (fresh-squeezed is best)
- 1 cup carrots, rough chopped
- large handful of kale
- large handful of spinach
- 1/4 cup fresh parsley
- 1 avocado

procedure:

Blend and enjoy!

Serves 2

pineapple celery frappé

Helyn's notes: I've always heard celery juice is good for lowering blood pressure, so I decided to do some research to find out why. This versatile veggie contains compounds called phthalides. These compounds provide health benefits by naturally relaxing the muscles in and around the walls of the arteries which cause those vessels to dilate, creating more space inside the arteries that permits the blood to flow at a lower pressure. In one instance, the father of a scientist at UCMC experienced a drop in his blood pressure from 158/96 to 118/82 after just one week of eating about four stalks a day. That's pretty impressive!

ingredients:

- 1 ½ cups celery juice
- 1 ½ cups coconut water
- 2 cups frozen pineapple chunks

procedure:

Blend and enjoy!

Serves 2

banana lemon green smoothie

Helyn's notes: In a word ... refreshing! This smoothie is a real thirst quencher. The kale amps the nutritional profile, and the banana adds just the right amount of sweetness to counter the sourness of the lemon juice. Pucker up!

ingredients:

- 2 frozen bananas
- ½ cup raw cashews
- handful fresh kale
- juice of one lemon
- 2 cups coconut water

procedure:

1. Blend the cashews and one cup of the coconut water until smooth.
2. Add the remaining ingredients and blend until smooth. Enjoy!

Serves 2

matcha tea orange shake

Helyn's notes: Matcha tea has so many health benefits! It contains a unique, potent class of antioxidants known as catechins, found in green tea, which aren't found in other foods. In particular, the catechin EGCg (epigallocatechin gallate) provides potent cancer-fighting properties. I enjoy matcha tea's vibrant green color and mild flavor. This shake is so creamy and smooth. You'll love it!

ingredients:

- 2 frozen bananas
- 1 whole orange, peeled (no seeds, please!)
- 1 Haas avocado
- 1 cup orange juice (fresh is best)
- 1 cup coconut water
- 1 tsp matcha green tea

procedure:

1. Blend and enjoy!

Serves 2

Let food be thy medicine...

90

I want to tell you a little bit more about matcha tea. What is matcha? It is a finely ground, bright emerald-green tea powder that has been the heart of the famous Japanese tea ceremony for over 900 years. The Buddhist monks honored matcha tea as a health elixir for its potential to heighten concentration and enhance metabolism, and it is known to produce a calm, mental alertness.

What about other green teas? Aren't they just as health-promoting? To test the hypothesis that matcha is more catechin-dense than other green teas, researchers from the University of Colorado Springs conducted a comparison study between matcha and other common green teas. The results were groundbreaking as the authors discovered that the concentration of EGCg available from drinking matcha is 137 times greater than the amount of EGCg available from a common green tea. That means you'd have to drink 137 cups of regular green tea to get the same antioxidant protection found in a cup of matcha!

tropical green smoothie

Helyn's notes: Greens galore! There's a ton of yummy flavor in this smoothie, which trumps the flavor of all the healthy greens. Lots of nutrients and great taste ... the ultimate combination.

ingredients:

- 2 frozen bananas
- 1 cup chopped frozen mango
- ½ cup chopped frozen pineapple
- ¼ cup coconut milk
- 1 can coconut water (about 2 cups)
- 1 large collard leaf, stem removed
- 4-5 leaves of lacinato kale (or any kale)
- large handful of baby spinach

procedure:

1. Blend and enjoy!
2. Top with some banana slices and coconut flakes if desired.

Serves 2

summer slushies & frappés

tutti frutti slushy

Helyn's notes: Don't you just love slushies? Even the word is fun to say ... slushy. Slushies remind me of being five years old. This slushy is so much fun, both visually and to drink! You just never know which color or flavor is going to find its way into your straw ... slurp!

ingredients:

~ for the pink layer
- 1 frozen banana
- 1 cup frozen raspberries
- 1 TBSP maca powder
- ½-1 cup coconut water

~ for the yellow/orange layer
- 1 frozen banana
- 1 cup frozen mango
- 1 TBSP hemp seeds
- ½ tsp turmeric (optional)
- ½-1 cup coconut water

~ for the green layer
- 2 frozen bananas
- 2 cups loosely packed spinach
- 1 whole lime, peeled
- ½-1 cup coconut water

procedure:

1. Place each layer's ingredients into a high powered blender and blend until smooth. Add enough coconut water to each to create a thick consistency. If you don't have a high powered blender, such as a Vitamix, you will need more fluid.
2. Rinse the blender between layers to keep the colors pure.
3. As you finish each layer, divide each batch into two 12 oz. glasses, layers one on top of another. Enjoy!

Serves 2

Oh, hi! Are you enjoying this smoothie book so far? Great! Please spread the word!

Thanks a ton!
I appreciate you!

kiwi lime slushy

Helyn's notes: This may very well be the most refreshing thing I've ever put in my mouth. Seriously revitalizing! It's a perfect way to cool off on a warm day. Filled with yummy goodness through and through. I'm calling it a kiwi lime slushy since those are the flavors that are most prominent. But it's also chock-full of honeydew melon (yum again) and frozen green grapes for a sweet-tart kick. A handful of fresh spinach leaves adds that bright green glow and some extra nutrients. Go ahead, cool your engines!

ingredients:

- 2 cups coconut water
- 1 heaping cup frozen green grapes
- 2 heaping cups frozen honeydew melon chunks
- 2 kiwis, peeled
- zest and flesh of one organic lime

procedure:

Blend and enjoy!

Serves 2

frozen lime slushy

Helyn's notes: Frozen grapes are once more the star of the show! I freeze them all the time in the summer. They make wonderful snacks, even on their own! Kick your thirst to the curb with this amazingly refreshing treat!

ingredients:

- 3 cups frozen green grapes (Make sure they're organic!)
- 1 large lime, peeled
- zest of the same lime
- 1 cup coconut water
- handful of ice

procedure:

Blend and enjoy!

Serves 2

fruity radish detox slushy

Helyn's notes: This is a refreshing and rejuvenating drink for a hot summer day or a perfect breakfast when you've overeaten or eaten heavy or unhealthy foods the day prior. One note: this smoothie is not for you if you don't care for radishes as they are the predominant flavor in this recipe. You can always reduce the amount of them for a fruitier taste if you prefer. I happen to love the crisp, peppery flavor of radishes! All of the ingredients in this smoothie have some kind of detoxification properties.

ingredients:

- 1 cup strawberries
- 2 cups chopped watermelon
- 1 cup chopped honeydew melon
- 1 banana
- 4 large red radishes
- 1 cup coconut water (use a little more or less to achieve desired consistency)

procedure:

Blend and enjoy!

Serves 2

pink grapefruit slushy

Helyn's notes: Grapefruits are one of my favorite types of citrus. I know that many people feel they are too sour, but my palate seems happy with their pucker power. Did you know that there are phytonutrients in grapefruit called limonoids? They inhibit tumor formation by promoting the production of glutathione-S-transferase, a detoxifying enzyme. This enzyme sparks a reaction in the liver that helps to make toxic compounds more water soluble for excretion from the body. The pulp of grapefruit contains compounds that may help prevent breast cancer.

NOTE: Grapefruits can interact with certain medications. If you are taking prescription medications, check with your doctor before eating grapefruits.

ingredients:

- 1 ruby red grapefruit, peeled and any seeds removed
- 1 cup frozen red grapes
- 1 cup frozen watermelon chunks
- 1 cup pure coconut water
- 1 tsp beet juice (optional and for color)

procedure:

Blend and enjoy!

Serves 2

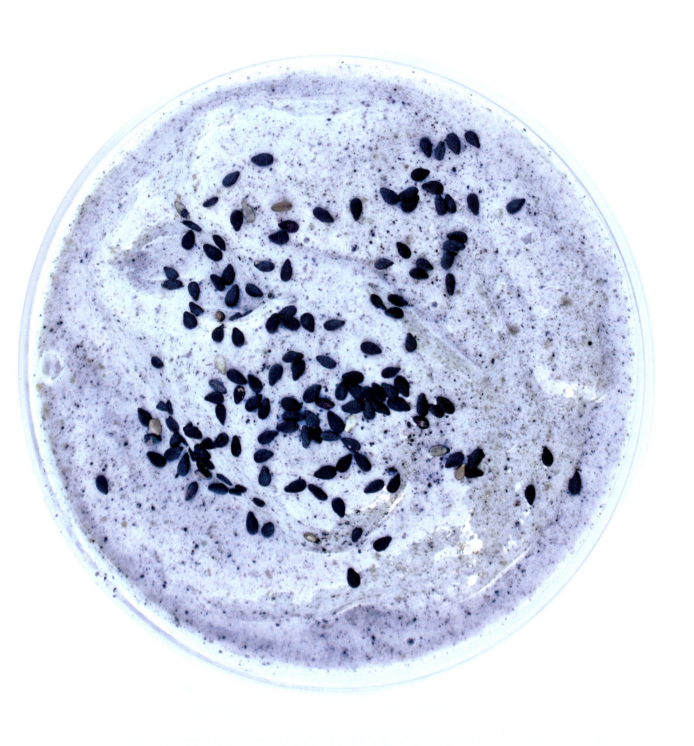

all shook-up elvis smoothie

Helyn's notes: I adore peanut butter and banana sandwiches! They were Elvis' signature sandwich. Of course, he also added bacon, which you can also enjoy with this sweet smoothie ... just follow my recipe for shiitake bacon on my blog to use as a garnish if you want the real deal!

ingredients:

~ the smoothie
- 3 frozen bananas
- 2 cups unsweetened, plant-based milk
- 1 cup ice
- ½ cup smooth peanut butter
- 4 pitted medjool dates
- 1 TBSP flax meal
- 1 tsp chia seeds

~ the garnishes
- ¼ cup smooth peanut butter
- 2 TBSP maple syrup or other liquid sweetener of your choice
- 1 fresh banana
- 3 TBSP chopped peanuts
- shiitake bacon strips (find recipe on my blog)

procedure:

1. Create the garnishes first if you're using them. Mix the ¼ cup peanut butter with the sweetener, and streak the insides of the serving glasses.
2. Chop the peanuts very fine.
3. Slice the banana and dredge in the chopped peanuts. Set aside.
4. Place all smoothie ingredients in a high powdered blender and blend until smooth.
5. Pour into the prepared glasses, and top with the peanut coated bananas. Finish with remaining chopped peanuts.

i'm in love...

Serves 2

v-12 vegetable juice smoothie

Helyn's notes: You can experiment with whatever veggies you like in a mixed veggie smoothie. I worked on this one for a while to get a similar flavor to traditional V-8 juice. Also, you can use either fresh tomatoes or tomato purée. I used purée, which also added more thickness. And there's just something about blending a tomato or tomato product which results in a lot of air in the smoothie, making it thicker! I guess what I'm saying is ... use a thick straw.

ingredients:

- 1 cup tomato purée (or 2 fresh tomatoes)
- 1 cucumber
- 1 carrot
- 1 red bell pepper
- 2 celery stalks
- 1 small red beet
- large handful kale
- large handful spinach
- large handful lettuce (any kind)
- 5-6 parsley stalks, stems included
- 1 green onion stalk
- juice of 1/2 lime (use the rest for garnish)

Add ins (optional and to taste):
- fresh or prepared horseradish
- tamari or other low-sodium soy sauce
- hot sauce

procedure:

Blend the high-water-content veggies together first, like the tomato, cucumber, and greens. Then add the others, rough-chopped. Blend until smooth.

Serves 2

holiday cranberry walnut smoothie

Helyn's notes: This smoothie has become one of my favorites in the winter months, and I'm sure you will love it, too. Fresh cranberries add a wonderful ZING while the walnuts smooth things out, and the sweetness is derived from bananas and o.j. Adding a date or two really compliments the tart cranberries!

ingredients:

- 3 frozen bananas
- 2 cups orange juice (fresh squeezed is best!)
- ½ cup raw walnuts
- 1 cup fresh cranberries
- 2 TBSP ground flax seeds
- 2 pitted medjool dates (optional)
- some chopped walnuts and a few cranberries for garnish

procedure:

1. Place all ingredients into a high-powered blender and blend until combined. I left mine just a little short of smooth with some bits of cranberry not totally blended.
2. Garnish with walnuts and cranberries if desired.

Serves 2

LET IT SNOW

black sesame shake

Helyn's notes: Intoxicatingly interesting and exotically flavorful is what I call this whole foods concoction. You've had tahini, no doubt, but have you ever tried BLACK tahini? You must. Made with black sesame seeds, it has a depth of flavor that is indescribable. Not sure of the nutrient content versus the traditional, brown sesame seed tahini. I searched the web and came up empty. But the flavor is decidedly unique.

ingredients:

- 2 frozen bananas
- 2 cups unsweetened, plant-based milk
- 1/4 cup black sesame tahini
- 4 pitted medjool dates
- 1 cup ice cubes
- 1 tsp toasted sesame oil (optional, but adds another dimension of flavor)

procedure:

Blend and enjoy!

Serves 2

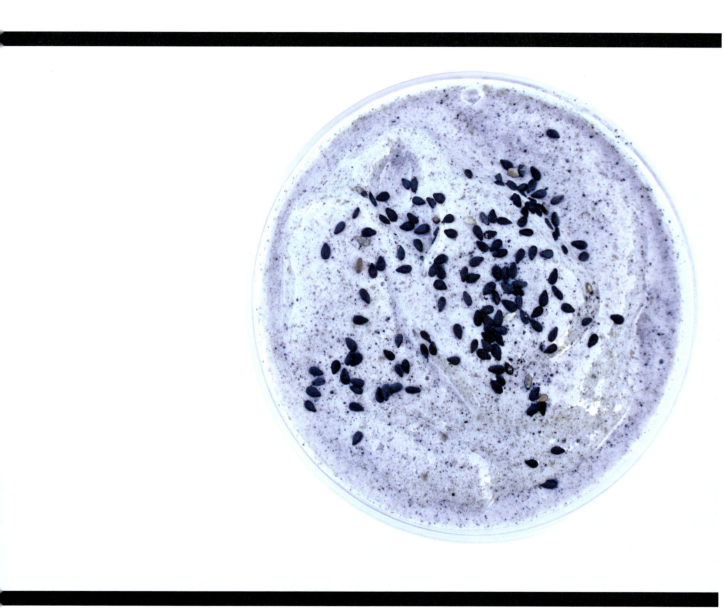

wickedly delicious halloween smoothie

Helyn's notes: Your kids will love these! Playing with lively colors is a great way to make many traditional foods into Halloween-worthy creations ... like this delicious and nutritious smoothie!

ingredients:

~ for the purple/red layer

- 1 frozen banana
- 1 cup frozen blueberries
- 1½ cups cherry or pomegranate juice

~ for the orange layer

- 1 frozen banana
- 1 cup frozen mango
- 1 carrot, chopped into 1" pieces
- 1 cup coconut water

~ for the green layer

- 1 frozen banana
- ½ cup frozen mango
- 1 cup chopped greens, such as spinach or kale (I used kale)
- 2 tsp green powder, such as powdered barley grass juice or spirulina
- 1 cup coconut water

procedure:

1. Blend each color's ingredients and set each aside.
2. Assemble your smoothie glasses pouring each color in on top of the other.
3. Swirl gently with a straw or knife to slightly blend the colors.

Serves 2

p.b.&j. smoothie

Helyn's notes: Who doesn't love the familiar flavor combination of peanut butter and jelly? I used strawberries for this smoothie, but use whatever fruits you like. This playful smoothie will awaken the kid in you and leave you wanting MORE!

ingredients:

~ for the peanut butter part
- 2 bananas
- 1/4 cup natural peanut butter
- 1 cup unsweetened, plant-based milk
- 2 TBSP flax meal

~ for the jelly part
- 2 cups fresh or frozen strawberries
- 3 pitted medjool dates
- 1 1/2 cups coconut water

procedure:

Blend each part separately, then layer and/or swirl in glasses. Enjoy!

Serves 2

 more, please!

carrot cake smoothie

Helyn's notes: Another blended taste sensation ... carrot cake! Wowee. This smoothie takes the cake ... :) I used my homemade cashew cream cheese for the topping, so plan ahead for this smoothie if you want to really enjoy the authentic flavors of carrot cake. Please don't break my heart and buy that totally processed vegan cream cheese crap. No.

ingredients:

- 2 frozen bananas
- 2 cups unsweetened, plant-based milk
- 2 cups rough-chopped carrots
- 1/2 cup raw walnuts
- 1/4 cup organic raisins
- 1/2 cup pitted medjool dates
- 1 TBSP chia seeds
- 1 tsp cinnamon
- 1/4 tsp ground nutmeg
- 1/8 tsp ground cloves
- 1/4 tsp turmeric (optional, adds a nice color and more nutrients)

~ toppings:
- 1/2 cup cashew cream cheese
- 2 TBSP maple syrup
- chopped walnuts
- shredded carrots

procedure:

1. Combine the cream cheese with the maple syrup, and set aside.
2. Blend all smoothie ingredients and pour into glasses.
3. Top with the cream cheese and the extra walnuts and carrots. Enjoy!

Serves 2

red velvet shake

Helyn's notes: Are you a fan of red velvet cake? Looking for a healthy alternative and a sweet dessert smoothie for your valentine? Here you go!

ingredients:

- 1 cup cooked, rough-chopped beets
- 1 frozen banana
- 1 1/2 cups unsweetened, plant-based milk
- 8 pitted medjool dates
- 1/4 cup cocoa powder
- 1 cup ice cubes
- 2 tsp pure vanilla extract

procedure:

1. Blend and enjoy

Serves 2

strawberry cheezecake smoothie

Helyn's notes: Another classic flavor fusion ... and another fanciful smoothie that you will need to prepare ahead for, using homemade cashew cream cheese again. I felt oddly guilty having this smoothie for breakfast. It was like having a slice of decadent cheesecake. Really! As I was enjoying the dozens of taste explosions in my mouth, I couldn't help pondering how silly it is that most meat eaters believe that vegans are somehow deprived. Ha! Hardly.

ingredients:

~ smoothie
- 2 cups frozen organic strawberries
- 2 cups unsweetened, plant-based milk
- ¼ cup vegan cream cheese
- 4 pitted medjool dates
- 2 tsp pure vanilla extract

~ "crust"
- ½ cup graham cracker crumbs. It's hard to say exactly how many crackers will make this much crumb. You'll have to guesstimate! Doesn't have to be precise. (It can be hard to find gluten-free grahams. Kinnikinnick brand makes one called S'moreables Graham Style Crackers which are sometimes in health food stores. If you aren't gluten-intolerant you can use Midel Honey Grahams which are 100% whole wheat.)
- 1 medjool date

~ topping
- 4 fresh, ripe, organic strawberries
- 1 TBSP strawberry fruit-sweetened spread (such as Polaner or St. Dalfour)

procedure:

1. Place graham crackers and 1 medjool date into food processor and pulse to a fine crumb.
2. Chop the fresh strawberries and mix with the fruit spread. Set aside.
3. Place all smoothie ingredients into a blender and blend until smooth.
4. Create layers of smoothie, crumbs, and strawberries as you would a parfait.
5. Serve with straws ... and spoons!

Serves 2

I hope you've enjoyed all of my smoothie recipes. They're yours now, too.

For more nourishing, plant-strong recipes visit:

www.helynskitchen.com

Healthy trails!

Lightning Source UK Ltd.
Milton Keynes UK
UKRC02n2149060717
304842UK00005B/55